WORSHIP
HONORING GOD IN ALL OF LIFE

FOUNDATIONS FOR
CHRISTIAN LIVING
SERIES

NAVPRESS
BRINGING TRUTH TO LIFE
NavPress Publishing Group
P.O. Box 35001, Colorado Springs, Colorado 80935

The Navigators is an international Christian organization. Our mission is to reach, disciple, and equip people to know Christ and to make Him known through successive generations. We envision multitudes of diverse people in the United States and every other nation who have a passionate love for Christ, live a lifestyle of sharing Christ's love, and multiply spiritual laborers among those without Christ.

NavPress is the publishing ministry of The Navigators. NavPress publications help believers learn biblical truth and apply what they learn to their lives and ministries. Our mission is to stimulate spiritual formation among our readers.

Cover photo by Randy Wells / Tony Stone Images

The FOUNDATIONS FOR CHRISTIAN LIVING (FCL) series grew out of The Navigators' worldwide Scriptural Roots of the Ministry (SRM) process. The eight guides in this series reflect the major themes that emerged from ten years of Scriptural study, international dialogue, and prayer. It is the desire of the SRM team that those who follow Jesus Christ be grounded in these fundamental elements of the faith. For more information regarding the SRM process, please write to NavPress at the above address. The FCL series was researched and developed by Don Bartel, John Purvis, and Chuck Steen. The series text was written by Joanne Heim.

Printed in the United States of America

1 2 3 4 5 6 7 8 9 10 11 12 13 14 15 / 02 01 00 99 98 97

CONTENTS

How to Use this Guide 5

SESSION ONE
Three Big Ideas 11

SESSION TWO
The Universe's Priority of Worship 21

SESSION THREE
The Revelation of God's Glory 31

SESSION FOUR
Our Response to God and His Glory 43

SESSION FIVE
Balancing Freedom and Order in Worship 53

SESSION SIX
Idols of the Heart 63

SESSION SEVEN
False Worship in the Community 73

SESSION EIGHT
Let's Personalize Worship 83

SESSION NINE
Let's Grow Together Through Worship 89

HOW TO USE THIS GUIDE

What comes into our minds when we think
about God is the most important thing about us.

—A.W. Tozer

Many people think of worship as individuals standing or sitting in rows for an hour or two a week. But there's far more to worship. Worship involves all of who we are, in every activity of our lives. Every human being possesses an inborn instinct to worship, and to the degree that we are not worshiping the true God with all our heart, soul, mind, and strength, we will inevitably worship other gods. This study offers you a chance both to connect in worship with the God of glory and to identify the idols that hinder you from cultivating such a worship connection hour by hour.

The FOUNDATIONS Process

The FOUNDATIONS series will help you not merely learn about God but also grow in your love for Him. Through the FOUNDATIONS process you'll grow in discovering God, experiencing one another, and serving in the world. Your group will . . .

- ▶ pursue the mystery of God together and discover ways to draw closer to Him
- ▶ grow as you learn to be honest and vulnerable with one another, deeply accepting one another
- ▶ become courageous in helping one another at the point of personal need
- ▶ discover how to live genuinely in this fast-paced, complex world
- ▶ design ways to serve God together, as a group

The nine sessions in this study follow a three-stage process:

1. Session 1 introduces you to the FOUNDATIONS series. You'll explore three essential elements of the spiritual life on which the series focuses. You'll also begin to develop relationships with the other people in your small group. Session 1 is the same in all FOUNDATIONS studies. If you have recently used another FOUNDATIONS study with your current group, you may simply review session 1 of this study.
2. Sessions 2 through 7 lead you through a variety of issues related to worshiping God in all of life.
3. Sessions 8 and 9 enable you to take stock of what you've studied and consider what you want to do about it. In session 8 you'll discern how the material applies to you as an individual. Your group will offer feedback and support in following through. In session 9 you'll discuss how the material applies to you as a group. Most of the Bible was written to groups of people rather than to individuals, so session 9 may bring your study alive in ways you did not expect. Session 9 will also help you assess your group's progress in becoming a community as you look at unity, intimacy, interdependence, and mission.

A Modular Approach
Each session is divided into four modules or sections.

OVERVIEW

The overview section briefly describes where the session is headed and what your goals will be. The key issue is stated in the paragraph labeled "So, what's the big deal?" This issue will normally be a point of tension between what the Bible teaches and what we commonly experience. The session will then help your group wrestle through that tension together.

Stating the key issue up front risks preempting the Holy Spirit from guiding your group in the direction He wants to take it, but if you remain open to His leading throughout your individual preparation and group meeting, we believe He'll use the material to minister to you in ways you wouldn't have imagined.

ON YOUR OWN **(30-60 minutes)**

This section includes the passages you should be sure to examine before your group meets. You'll find some questions easy; others will stretch you mentally. We've found that a spiritual person is defined more by the internal questions he or she is asking than by the conclusions he or she has already reached. Mind-stretching questions are ideal for group discussion—be prepared for a lively debate!

As you work through this material, it will be helpful to remember a few "principles of understanding" that relate to learning about God:

▶ Understanding comes through mental exertion (Proverbs 2:3-5). Make sure you schedule enough preparation time to delve into the topic.

▶ Understanding comes through the soul and spirit (John 4:24). Seek God in your spirit as you study, as well as when you discuss.

▶ Understanding comes through the insight of others (Romans 1:12; Acts 17:11). Ask God to make you discerning so you will hear what He is saying to you through each other.

GROUP DISCOVERY **(40-90 minutes)**

This will be the discussion portion of your group meeting. It will usually include three sub-sections:

Let's Warm Up: Each group session opens with a question or two to help you learn about each other. The warm-up questions also help you move from what you were thinking about (or worried about) when you arrived at the meeting to what the biblical texts deal with. These questions put you in touch with the topic in an experiential way, so your discussion is not just sharing ideas but sharing life. The questions in this section always focus on life experiences and are usually fun to answer.

Let's Talk: In this section you'll examine one or two key Bible passages on the topic and discuss what light these passages shed on the central tension of the study. You'll also discuss any questions raised by your individual study. Feel free to bring to the group anything that perplexed or excited you in your individual study.

Let's Act: The questions in this section connect what you've studied to how you live. They often ask you to consider applying what you've learned to your group as a whole, rather than just to your individual life. Application is the reason for Bible study; be sure you allow plenty of time for it.

♥ GROUP WORSHIP (15-30 minutes)

In order to stress the importance of the worship portion of your meeting, we have set it apart as a special section. Worship and prayer as a group are essential components of the FOUNDATIONS process. Praying and worshiping together can be one of the most faith-building and relationship-building activities you do together. Since many people have never prayed aloud with others before, the suggestions for worship begin gently. Later in the study you'll have an opportunity to plan your own worship times. You may decide to assign one person in the group to plan and lead worship, or you may rotate the responsibility.

In session 4 you'll begin to set aside at least 15 minutes of your worship time to discuss prayerfully and humbly a question often over-looked in Bible studies: "What is the Holy Spirit saying to us?" (This is referred to as *Let's Listen to God*.) You may find it challenging to get past what you imagine God ought to be saying to the group. The experience of trying to discern God's voice will invariably draw your group to a deeper level of intimacy.

Facilitator's Job Description

Leadership is essential to an effective group. FOUNDATIONS studies will go much better if someone in your group takes responsibility to:

1. Launch the group
   ▶ Recruit people for the group, explaining its purpose and process.
   ▶ Schedule meetings (with group consensus).

2. Pray regularly
   ▶ For the individual members in their daily lives.
   ▶ For the group's growth into community.
   ▶ For the courage and faith of the group to take the steps it needs
     to grow in Christ.

3. Build community
   ▶ Stay in touch with the members, encouraging them to also stay
     in touch with each other.
   ▶ Make sure that each member grows in his or her ownership of
     this group. (This can be done by assigning responsibility—those
     with responsibility usually experience ownership and genuine
     membership in a group.)
   ▶ Help the group move beyond studying to doing.
   ▶ Maintain momentum and remotivate group members if
     enthusiasm diminishes.

4. Facilitate rather than lead
   ▶ Search for vision and direction together, rather than announcing
     vision and answers. Help the group arrive at its vision and
     answers. Help people go where the Spirit is leading them,
     rather than where you think they should go. Remind them that
     understanding is only the beginning; implementing is the goal.
   ▶ Teach by asking questions, rather than making authoritative
     statements. Questions can often accomplish what statements
     cannot. Questions were Jesus' preferred style.
   ▶ Draw out the quiet or introverted persons.
   ▶ Encourage everyone's participation; affirm the different
     contributions of all.

5. Be content with less than ideal progress
   ▶ Put up with some ambiguity. People never grow in a constant or
     straight line. Two steps forward and one step back is the norm.
     Remember what Christ has tolerated in you. Be happy with
     progress in the general direction of FOUNDATIONS goals.

6. Watch the clock
   ▶ When the allotted time for a given section is over, go on to the

next section even if the group has not exhausted its discussion. (It is likely you will need to do this—many of the **Let's Talk** sections have more than enough material to fill the recommended time slot.) Unless you have unlimited time, the group will appreciate being kept on schedule. Don't allow discussion to consume all of your time so that application and worship must be omitted. On the other hand, if you sense the Spirit of God is actively at work, follow the Spirit's leading, not the clock. Look for an appropriate time at which to say, "I sense that God is doing something important here. Is it okay with all of you if we extend our time in this section of the meeting?"

7. Delegate
   ► After the first two or three sessions, ask someone else in the group to lead the worship time. Someone in your group is probably gifted in the area of worship and interested in helping the group focus on God through worship. Also, ask someone to lead the Group Discovery discussion. Direct that person to read item 4 in this job description. You could rotate this job around the group. Finally, appoint someone else to be timekeeper. By delegating these three functions, you will encourage all participants to feel like owners of the group rather than spectators.

3. Establish ground rules
   ► It is important that everyone in the group has a chance to buy into the rules by which the group will run. Ground rules clarify what the group expects from each person. The most important ground rules are stated on pages 17-18. Be sure to discuss them in your first meeting.

1.

THREE BIG IDEAS

In this introductory session you'll examine the three essential elements of the spiritual life on which the FOUNDATIONS series focuses: worship, community, and service. Your goals will be:

▶ To understand and own these three elements—worship, community, and service
▶ To get to know each other by telling a little of your stories and why you've joined this group

Session 1 is the same in all FOUNDATIONS studies. If you have recently used another FOUNDATIONS study with your current group, you may choose to do session 1 or merely to review it and then skip to session 2.

ON YOUR OWN   (30-60 minutes)

Most of us would like to love and be loved better than we already do and are. The FOUNDATIONS series revolves around three fundamental commands Jesus gave to His followers:

▶ Love God with all your heart, soul, mind, and strength (see Mark 12:30).
▶ Love one another as Jesus loves you (see John 13:34).
▶ Love your neighbor as yourself (see Mark 12:31).

In these verses, Jesus states the "big picture" of what the spiritual life is about. We love Him through worship, we love one another through

11

community, and we love others through service. We can depict this threefold lifestyle with the following set of concentric circles:

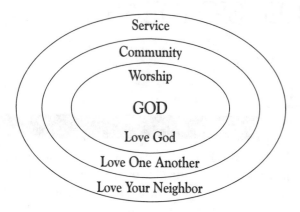

These three commands may be summarized in a single goal for the series:

To help you become a community—a small, closely knit group motivated and empowered to worship and serve God together.

Worship, community, and service form the structural backbone of the FOUNDATIONS process. They will direct your love toward God, toward the others in your group, and toward your neighbors (others not yet a part of your group). At the end of this study, you'll have a chance to summarize what you've learned about worship, community, and service, and to assess your progress as a group toward these three outcomes.

WORSHIP

God's commands about love show that He is vitally interested in relationships and that our relationship with Him should be our highest priority. Worship is the all-consuming, ongoing activity of heaven. We have the inexpressible privilege of joining in the cosmic worship of the King already taking place in the heavenly realm.

When we see God as He is and worship Him, the other areas of our lives begin to work themselves out. Drawing near to God's heart in spirit and truth will inevitably affect our relationships with others.

Hence, worship will become the centerpiece of your group experience. This concentration on God will set your little community apart from a mere discussion group or gathering of friends. While early sessions of this study will include suggestions for worship, feel free to use your entire group's creativity and experience under the leadership of the Holy Spirit as you come into God's presence session by session.

The essence of worship is turning our attention toward God, reflecting His glorious attributes back to Him, and agreeing with who He is and what He has done. God delights to reveal Himself more fully to us as we worship, to satisfy our hearts' desire for relationship with Him, and to give us help for our desperate needs.

God invites us to come to Him with our burdens, needs, joys, and heartaches. In reality, we cannot come to God without our burdens; they are part of who we are. Instead of denying the things on our hearts, we'll find it far more helpful to acknowledge them as fully as possible, commit them to God, then seek Him in His greatness for who He is.

1. When you think of worship, what ideas or images come to mind?
   ☐ lively music
   ☐ majestic hymns or choral works
   ☐ silence and solitude
   ☐ lengthy sermons
   ☐ performers and spectators
   ☐ communing with nature in the woods or by a stream
   ☐ all of life
   ☐ other:

2. On a scale of 1 to 10, how would you rate your most recent experience of worship in terms of how well it focused your heart on God's greatness? Why?

1	2	3	4	5	6	7	8	9	10
dry				okay					awesome

3. Does the idea of worship being the centerpiece of your group experience attract or trouble you? Why?

COMMUNITY

From a centered place of loving God, you'll move outward to loving the others in your group. This shared life is what the New Testament writers mean by *koinonia*: "fellowship," "communion," "partnership," "participation," "community."

> We saw it, we heard it, and now we're telling you so you can experience it along with us, this experience of communion with the Father and his Son, Jesus Christ. Our motive for writing is simply this: We want you to enjoy this, too. Your joy will double our joy! (1 John 1:3-4, MSG)

In the FOUNDATIONS series we assume that dynamic Christian community as described in the New Testament is not only possible but normative for us. When we fail to experience such relationships, we miss the fullness of life that God intends for us. While there are many spiritually important things one can and should do alone, an effective community contributes equally crucial ingredients of life. People in community can:

- ▶ encourage one another in good times and bad
- ▶ ask thoughtful questions when a member has a decision to make
- ▶ listen to God together
- ▶ learn how to pray together and for one another
- ▶ benefit from one another's insights into Scripture
- ▶ acquire a habit of reading the Bible
- ▶ practice loving their neighbors
- ▶ worship God together
- ▶ learn to communicate effectively and solve problems together
- ▶ learn to receive care from others
- ▶ experience the pleasure of helping another person grow

Community in these studies refers to a small group of 3 to 13 people who relate in a certain way. Community in this sense is very different from any organizational form or structure. Matthew 18:20 says, "For where there are two or three who have been joined together into my Name with the result that I am the common object of their faith, there I am in their midst."[1] The individuals together are seeking intimacy with God and fellowship with each other. *Koinonia* includes partnership, participation, and contribution. It implies communication and vulnerability. It is much more than just getting together and discussing some nonvolatile topic.

Jesus wanted His disciples to experience a unique relationship when they came together—unique in their love for and their unity with one another. When genuine love is present, a group has taken the first and biggest step toward real community. This process is not easy. Your group will probably have to resolve a number of relational issues on the road to biblical community.

4. What appeals to you about this description of community?

5. What questions or concerns do you have about this kind of community? Explain.

SERVICE

Any community focused on God loves to serve both believers and unbelievers, just as God does. How could it be otherwise? You'll find that as your group grows in worshiping God and loving one another, the members will intuitively know they need to be helping others. This will be natural.

What may not be natural is serving together as a team and serving the lost—both of which Jesus did and which His followers throughout history have done.

Most of us slowly abandon former friends and acquaintances when we join the kingdom of God. We're not comfortable anymore around those who do not share our new values. Our old friends no longer feel comfortable around us. Somehow we lose the ability Jesus had to be "a friend of tax collectors and 'sinners'" (Matthew 11:19). It is far easier for us to serve those within the kingdom of God than those more distant.

And if somehow we do seek to draw the lost toward Christ, we usually do so as individuals, rather than in partnership with other believers. Consequently, those who need the Savior never experience the powerful influence of a loving community.

The FOUNDATIONS studies will guide your group into these two dimensions: serving the lost and serving together. Serving does not exclusively mean explaining the gospel verbally. Loving our neighbor often translates into specific acts of compassionate service at home, neighborhood, or work. We often serve individually, but this FOUNDATIONS guide will focus your efforts on serving God's interests together. You will not be told what to do; you will not be pushed beyond your point of willing consent. Rather, you will decide together how to put what you are studying into practice outside your group.

6. What thoughts and feelings does this description of service raise for you?
   ☐ Excitement—I'm ready to go!
   ☐ Discomfort—The last thing I need is more on my "to-do" list.
   ☐ Anxiety—I did door-to-door witnessing several years ago and hated it. Will we have to do that again?
   ☐ Ambivalence—I have a strong desire to serve more, but I know it's not easy for me.
   ☐ Confusion—Isn't it good enough for us just to take care of each other for awhile?
   ☐ Relief—I'm glad this isn't just another navel-gazing group.
   ☐ Other (explain):

7. Is this statement true of you: "It is far easier for us to serve those within the kingdom of God than those more distant." If so, why do you think that is?

8. We have stated three priorities: loving God, loving others in the group, and loving others outside the group. What about loving yourself? Do you think this should be a priority ahead of any or all of these three? Explain your view.

 GROUP DISCOVERY (40-90 minutes)

Let's Warm Up (10 minutes)

Beginning with the leader, let each person take one minute to answer question 9.

9. Recall an important friendship from your childhood. Who was that friend, and what was special about that friendship? What bond kept you and that friend together?

Let's Talk (30 minutes)

10. Share your responses to questions 1-8 in the "On Your Own" section. Discuss any questions you have about the three big ideas stated there.

11. Discuss the following ground rules for your group. Feel free to change anything. The objective is for everyone to be content with the result, not for everyone to go along while harboring private reservations.

☐ Purpose: The reason our group exists is to become a community—a small, closely knit group motivated and empowered to worship and serve God.

☐ Participation: I am committed to participating in this community, to worshiping, and to serving others outside the group.

☐ Attendance: I will be here as often as possible. This group will be a priority.

☐ Ownership: I agree to share responsibility for our group goals.

☐ Confidentiality: I agree to keep here whatever is shared here.

☐ Accountability: I agree to give permission to the other group members to hold me accountable for goals I set for myself.

☐ Accessibility: I give group members permission to call me when they are in need—even in the middle of the night. My phone number is. . . .

GROUP WORSHIP   (15-30 minutes)

12. Pray that God would begin to reveal Himself in more of His majesty, power, and direction.

13. Read aloud together this portion of Psalm 89 (from *The Message*):

Your love, GOD, is my song, and I'll sing it!
    I'm forever telling everyone how faithful you are.
I'll never quit telling the story of your love—
    how you built the cosmos
    and guaranteed everything in it.
Your love has always been our lives' foundation,
    your fidelity has been the roof over our world.
You once said, "I joined forces with my chosen leader,
    I pledged my word to my servant, David, saying,
'Everyone descending from you is guaranteed life;
    I'll make your rule as solid and lasting as rock.'"

GOD! Let the cosmos praise your wonderful ways,
    the choir of holy angels sing anthems to your faithful ways!
Search high and low, scan skies and land,
    you'll find nothing and no one quite like GOD.
The holy angels are in awe before him;
    he looms immense and august over everyone around him.
GOD of the Angel Armies, who is like you,
    powerful and faithful from every angle?
You put the arrogant ocean in its place
    and calm its waves when they turn unruly.

You gave that old hag Egypt the back of your hand,
  you brushed off your enemies with a flick of your wrist.
You own the cosmos—you made everything in it,
  everything from atom to archangel.
You positioned the North and South Poles;
  the mountains Tabor and Hermon sing duets to you.
With your well-muscled arm and your grip of steel—
  nobody trifles with you!
The Right and Justice are the roots of your rule;
  Love and Truth are its fruits.
Blessed are the people who know the passwords of praise,
  who shout on parade in the bright presence of GOD.
Delighted, they dance all day long; they know
  who you are, what you do—they can't keep it quiet!
Your vibrant beauty has gotten inside us—
  you've been so good to us! We're walking on air!
All we are and have we owe to GOD,
  Holy God of Israel, our King! (Psalm 89:1-18, MSG)

14. Allow a moment of silence for everyone to focus on God. In
worship, you have no agenda but to focus on Him.

15. Beginning with the leader, let each person thank God for one thing
he or she learned in this session, or praise God for one aspect of
Himself highlighted in your discussion. If you are comfortable doing
so, allow for additional, spontaneous expressions of thanks and praise.

Optional
If you think your group might appreciate singing together, ask someone
to lead with guitar or other instrument. If no one in your group has that
skill, consider singing with a CD; some are now designed especially for
small group worship. Be sure the person who leads worship understands
that singing is only one aspect of worship, and that he or she should limit
singing to the time allotted in your schedule.

---

1. Wuest, Kenneth S. *The New Testament: An Expanded Translation.*
Grand Rapids, Mich.: Eerdmans, 1961.

2.
THE UNIVERSE'S PRIORITY OF WORSHIP

Worship shapes the human community in response to the Living God. If worship is neglected or perverted, our communities fall into chaos or under tyranny.

—Eugene Peterson

OVERVIEW

When your group gathers for worship, you may feel you're alone in a room doing your thing. In reality, you are worshiping within the larger context of all humanity, even the cosmos, worshiping the living God.

Worship is like a giant whirlpool, catching up the whole of creation in its currents. Nearest the center, where God is, the currents are strongest. Far from the center we feel the turbulence and moral chaos created by sin. As the integrating center, God is the focus of everything surrounding Him, and He draws everything toward Himself. As we are drawn toward the center in worship, we realize that the powerful source of the whirlpool is deep down beneath what we see on the surface. Beneath the surface there is much more.

Likewise, in worship the whole of creation, especially humankind, focuses attention on God and draws closer to His person and into His presence. In this session we will get a glimpse of heavenly worship as the book of Revelation describes it, and contrast that picture with the ways most of us live and worship. Your goal as a group will be to wrestle with this tension between the worship you're made for and the quality of worship you actually live.

So what's the big deal?

God is the only valid focus of worship. To make anything else the object of worship is idolatry. Worship involves putting off our affections for idols and refocusing those affections on God.

ON YOUR OWN   (30-60 minutes)

The book of Revelation is a visionary letter from the apostle John to some severely persecuted Christians. He is perhaps over eighty years old when he writes this letter, describing a series of visions he has had of the war in heaven. In this ongoing battle between good and evil, God and those saints who overcome by faith will triumph.

1. Carefully read Revelation 4–5, which draws heavily on images borrowed from Old Testament passages, such as Genesis 49:8-12, Ezekiel 1:1-28, Daniel 7:10, and Zechariah 7:10. Pay careful attention to the sights, sounds, colors, movements, scope, furnishings, and space.

2. Project yourself into this heavenly worship service. Open up all five senses, plus your sanctified imagination.

   ☐ What do you see?

   ☐ Hear?

   ☐ Smell?

   ☐ Feel?

3. What object(s) stand out as most significant in this setting?

4. Who are the worshipers? (How many groups can you find?)

5. What postures or expressions of worship do you note in this heavenly service?

6. What is unique about the believer's role and privilege before God (5:9-10)?

7. Picture yourself as a news reporter attending this event. Write a headline and the opening paragraph for your paper. (What would distinguish your vision of heavenly creatures from those who claim to see alien creatures?)

8. Revelation 4–5 portrays how you will one day be worshiping God. How would you like this to influence the way you worship God now?

☐ I'm more motivated to clean up my act and persevere until the end.

☐ I'd love to worship that way, but it seems so out of place where I usually worship.

☐ I like worship to be physical: falling down before God, throwing crowns, etc.

☐ Color, music, light—worship should be beautiful.

☐ I want to maintain the sense of awe I get when I read this.

☐ The total focus on God is what I would like to adopt.

☐ Other (please explain):

9. What prevents you from worshiping God more fully, more frequently?

10. What can you use from this study on your own that will enhance the worship experience of your group?

For your group meeting, you will need your checkbook, calendar, and most recent credit card statement(s). You won't have to show these to anyone, but you will need to consult them personally.

In your group meeting, you'll compare the quality of worship in Revelation to the quality of worship in our daily lives. It's not easy to be honest about the things one worships. Such honesty requires trust. The following guidelines will help you build trust in your group:

- ▶ **Listen attentively.** Ask questions only to enhance understanding. It is more important for an individual to express himself than for the group to understand fully.
- ▶ **Respect the boundaries and comfort level of the one sharing.** If details that you are dying to know don't come out, be willing to die. Allow the person sharing to choose the amount of information he or she discloses.
- ▶ **Allow for the expression of emotions.** Have a box of tissues available. If someone cries, don't be too quick to change the mood. Give adequate time for the person to compose and continue.
- ▶ **Do not exhort, give advice, or teach.** This is not a counseling session, but an opportunity for group members to share deep, inner feelings and responses with friends. Nothing will shut down a group like someone offering advice at such a time.
- ▶ Always *affirm* the person who has shared.

It cannot be overemphasized that each person has a vital contribution to make to the group. For example, reflective people are important because they usually crystallize the group's ideas for deeper understanding. Talkative people generate dialogue and create an atmosphere of free expression.

Moreover, people are often blind to their deeper needs. They need the interaction and feedback of different kinds of people in the group to clearly understand these needs. Different people will help in different ways to illuminate and resolve these needs.

 GROUP DISCOVERY   **(50-90 minutes)**

Let's Warm Up (10 minutes)

Open with prayer that focuses on the issue raised in the paragraph, "So what's the big deal?" on page 22.

11. What was one of the most meaningful worship experiences you've had in the past year, and what made it so?

Let's Talk (30-50 minutes)

When used as a verb, worship means: (a) to like or enjoy enthusiastically, often excessively; (b) to honor in religious worship; (c) to regard with great awe and devotion; to regard with ardent or adoring esteem or devotion.

12. Take a couple of minutes on your own to list some of the things you "worship." Then share with the group what you learned about yourself.
    ☐ I adore . . .
    ☐ I am infatuated with . . .
    ☐ I celebrate . . .
    ☐ I dote upon . . .
    ☐ I idolize . . .
    ☐ I revel in . . .
    ☐ I sing the praises of . . .

The noun *worship* can mean either: (a) the "reverent love and devotion accorded a deity"; or (b) the "deep and often immoderate affection, devotion, or adoration" accorded an idol. All humans focus their worship on something or several things to the extent that they do not worship the living God. We are innately religious and will inevitably worship other gods, if not the living God.

13. Take a few minutes to glance through your calendar, checkbook, and credit card statement(s). Judging from the priorities reflected there, what other than God do you most worship with your time, money, and energy?

14. In the traditional religious sense of the word, when or how during the week do you "worship" God?

15. Revelation's glimpses of heavenly worship are meant to influence our current expressions of worship. From your study of Revelation 4–5, what seems to be the big idea that grabs your attention?

16. What goes on inside your head and heart when you hold these two things in tension:
    ☐ Christ on the throne, as described in Revelation 4–5
    ☐ Yourself somewhere near the throne, as reflected in your calendar, checkbook, and credit card statements

Let's Act (15-30 minutes)
In this section, think about how biblical truth from this session relates to you corporately, not just individually.

17. The images in Revelation 4–5 describe heavenly worship and expand our ideas of what worship can be here and now. How can your insights from this passage enliven your here-and-now worship life?

18. What does worship have to do with your relationships within this community?

19. How do your relationships affect the quality of your worship?

20. What does worship have to do with your relationships outside this community (neighbors, coworkers, family, new believers, mentors, enemies)?

21. Have you read or discussed anything in this session that will impact your worship of God?

GROUP WORSHIP   (15-30 minutes)

22. Reread the following choruses of praise from your study (Revelation 4:9-11; 5:9-10,12-13). This time read them aloud as a choral response to what God has revealed of Himself to you. Pause after every few phrases to allow anyone to comment on or pray about what was read. Especially focus on the character of God and His works.

Whenever the living creatures give glory, honor and thanks to him who sits on the throne and who lives for ever and ever, the twenty-four elders fall down before him who sits on the throne, and worship him who lives for ever and ever. They lay their crowns before the throne and say:

"You are worthy, our Lord and God,
    to receive glory and honor and power,
for you created all things,
    and by your will they were created
    and have their being." (Revelation 4:9-11)

And they sang a new song:

"You are worthy to take the scroll
    and to open its seals,
because you were slain,
    and with your blood you purchased men for God
from every tribe and language and people and nation.
You have made them to be a kingdom and priests to
    serve our God,
    and they will reign on the earth."

In a loud voice they sang:

"Worthy is the Lamb, who was slain,
to receive power and wealth and wisdom and strength
    and honor and glory and praise!"

Then I heard every creature in heaven and on earth and under the earth and on the sea, and all that is in them, singing:

"To him who sits on the throne and to the Lamb
be praise and honor and glory and power,
    for ever and ever!" (Revelation 5:9-10,12-13)

23. Your group may want to sing some praise songs based on one of these passages in Revelation.

24. Using language from Revelation 4–5, tell God why He is worthy of your worship more than any of the idols you identified in question 2.

25. If this discussion has raised questions about your priorities in worship, you might want to ask for the group's support in prayer. Spend a few minutes interceding with God on behalf of each other's shared concerns. Pray for each other to faithfully pull your affections away from other gods and place them fully on the one true God.

3.
THE REVELATION OF GOD'S GLORY

The chief end of man is to glorify God and enjoy Him forever.

> —Westminster Shorter Catechism

So whether you eat or drink or whatever you do, do it all for the glory of God.

> —the apostle Paul

OVERVIEW

Paul's whatever-you-do statement is a guiding principle to the person who struggles to pay the bills, to the person struggling to meet conflicting demands between work and home—to everyone who earnestly desires to serve God day by day. But what exactly is the glory of God, anyway?

In this session, we explore what God's glory is and how He reveals it. This survey of God's glory will span the full length of the Bible. Your goal will be to understand what God's glory is and how it is relevant to you.

So what's the big deal?

God's glory is a difficult concept to grasp. However, it's an essential one if we're going to understand how to respond to God in worship.

1. Using your own words, write a short paragraph defining or describing the "glory of God," as you understand the term. Ask yourself this question again at the end of this session after you've had the benefit of a careful Bible study.

As you read the passages in this study, use your imagination to picture the various scenes. Pay careful attention to the sights, sounds, smells, scope, and space that are associated with God's glory.

> The heavens declare the glory of God;
> > the skies proclaim the work of his hands.
> Day after day they pour forth speech;
> > night after night they display knowledge.
> There is no speech or language
> > where their voice is not heard.
> Their voice goes out into all the earth,
> > their words to the ends of the world.
> > (Psalm 19:1-4)

2. What do you think this psalmist means by God's glory?

3. How do the heavens show forth God's glory?

God had been revealing His glory to humans long before Israel became a nation. But when He called an oppressed band of people out of Egypt and forged them into a nation through many trials and much suffering, God revealed His glory visibly. The book of Exodus records what took place when Moses led the Israelites through the desert.

4. Read Exodus 16:6-10, 33:18-23, and 40:34-38. How did God reveal His glory in these three situations? (Note what you would have seen, heard, felt, and tasted if you had been on the scene for these events.)

Several hundred years later, the prophet Ezekiel had a vision of God's glory that continues to shock readers because it reads like science fiction. The four living creatures you read about in Revelation 4 formed a glowing, hovering expanse supporting a throne. Here is what Ezekiel saw on that throne:

> Then there came a voice from above the expanse over their [the living creatures'] heads as they stood with lowered wings. Above the expanse over their heads was what looked like a throne of sapphire, and high above on the throne was a figure like that of a man. I saw that from what appeared to be his waist up he looked like glowing metal, as if full of fire, and that from there down he looked like fire; and brilliant light surrounded him.

Like the appearance of a rainbow in the clouds on a rainy day, so was the radiance around him.

This was the appearance of the likeness of the glory of the LORD. When I saw it, I fell facedown, and I heard the voice of one speaking. (Ezekiel 1:25-28)

5. a. How did Ezekiel experience God's glory?

b. How did he respond to this awesome sight?

c. Why do you think he did that?

d. What do you make of this vision?

e. What does it add to your understanding of God's glory?

6. In these passages from Exodus and Ezekiel, God's glory means:
   ☐ God's beauty and perfection of character
   ☐ God's visible and active presence with His often-oppressed people
   ☐ Good reputation, high praise, justifiable honor
   ☐ Heavenly state of eternal bliss
   ☐ Material elegance or brilliance
   ☐ Other (please explain):

7. When and how does God make His glory known to humans?

8. How does God expect His people to respond to His revealed glory?

9. Do you get the impression that this vision of God's glory was unique to Moses and Ezekiel, or is it something all believers can experience? Why do you say that?

In light of all that the Old Testament revealed about God's glory, John made a startling claim in his Gospel.

> The Word became flesh and made his dwelling among us. We have seen his glory, the glory of the One and Only, who came from the Father, full of grace and truth. John testifies concerning him. He cries out, saying, "This was he of whom I said, 'He who comes after me has surpassed me because he was before me.'" From the fullness of his grace we have all received one blessing after another. For the law was given through Moses; grace and truth came through Jesus Christ. No one has ever seen God, but God the One and Only, who is at the Father's side, has made him known. (John 1:14-18)

10. The word for "dwelling" among us (John 1:14) literally means to tabernacle or tent among us. By drawing comparisons between God's glory revealed in Jesus and God's glory revealed in the Tent of Meeting with Moses (Exodus 40:34-35, John 1:17), what is John implying?

11. How would you define glory now?

12. God's glory is a difficult concept to grasp. What questions would you like to ask God about His glory?

 GROUP DISCOVERY (50-90 minutes)

Let's Warm Up (10 minutes)

13. After finishing her other morning routines, Susan sat down to her usual breakfast of cold cereal, hot coffee, and a hasty glance through the morning paper. Susan had every intention of having her daily quiet time with God, but as she moved from the breakfast table to her favorite reading chair, with her Bible and prayer journal in hand, something happened. She began to think about God and to pray about the people and things in her life, and then. . . . Complete this story for the group as if it were happening to you. Take a minute or two each.

Let's Talk (30 to 50 Minutes)

14. a. What did you learn about God's glory from your homework study?

b. What questions did it raise for you?

On the night before His death, Jesus offered a prayer to the Father of glory. He let His followers listen, so that they would know what was on His heart. Read John 17:1-26 carefully, underlining or highlighting references to "glory" and "glorifying."

> After Jesus said this, he looked toward heaven and prayed:
> "Father, the time has come. Glorify your Son, that your Son may glorify you. For you granted him authority over all people that he might give eternal life to all those you have given him. Now this is eternal life: that they may know you, the only true God, and Jesus Christ, whom you have sent. I have brought you glory on earth by completing the work you gave me to do. And now, Father, glorify me in your presence with the glory I had with you before the world began.
> "I have revealed you to those whom you gave me out of the world. They were yours; you gave them to me and they have obeyed your word. Now they know that everything you have given me comes from you. For I gave them the words you gave me and they accepted them. They knew with certainty that I came from you, and they believed that you sent me. I pray for them. I am not praying for the world, but for those you have given me, for they are yours. All I have is yours, and all you have is mine. And glory has come to me through them. I will remain in the world no longer, but they are still in the world, and I am coming to you. Holy Father, protect them by the power of your name—the name you gave me—so that they may be one as we are one. While I was with them, I protected them and kept them safe by that name you

gave me. None has been lost except the one doomed to destruction so that Scripture would be fulfilled.

"I am coming to you now, but I say these things while I am still in the world, so that they may have the full measure of my joy within them. I have given them your word and the world has hated them, for they are not of the world any more than I am of the world. My prayer is not that you take them out of the world but that you protect them from the evil one. They are not of the world, even as I am not of it. Sanctify them by the truth; your word is truth. As you sent me into the world, I have sent them into the world. For them I sanctify myself, that they too may be truly sanctified.

"My prayer is not for them alone. I pray also for those who will believe in me through their message, that all of them may be one, Father, just as you are in me and I am in you. May they also be in us so that the world may believe that you have sent me. I have given them the glory that you gave me, that they may be one as we are one: I in them and you in me. May they be brought to complete unity to let the world know that you sent me and have loved them even as you have loved me.

"Father, I want those you have given me to be with me where I am, and to see my glory, the glory you have given me because you loved me before the creation of the world.

"Righteous Father, though the world does not know you, I know you, and they know that you have sent me. I have made you known to them, and will continue to make you known in order that the love you have for me may be in them and that I myself may be in them." (John 17:1-26)

15. a. How do the Father and the Son bring glory to each other?

b. How do we bring glory to the Son?

c. How does Jesus give us the glory that God gave Him?

d. How will we see the glory of Christ?

16. So what? What does Jesus' prayer add to your understanding of God's glory?

17. As you try to digest all this information about God's glory, what are you feeling?
    - ☐ Bewildered, like straining to see through a thick fog.
    - ☐ Exhilarated, as though I've been climbing a mountain and am getting my first glimpse of the view from up here.
    - ☐ Dopey, as though I have jet lag and am not sure where my plane landed.
    - ☐ Awestruck, as though I'm really seeing God for the first time.
    - ☐ Frustrated, as though I'm trying to decipher the IRS tax code.
    - ☐ Other:

18. What would you like to say to God right now?

Let's Act (15-30 minutes)
In this section, think about how biblical truth from this session relates to you corporately, not just individually.

19. How is what you have learned about God's glory relevant to your worship and your relationship to God?

20. How does what you have learned about God's glory affect your relationships with each other?

21. How does it apply to your responsibilities and relationships with people outside the group—neighbors, coworkers, family, seekers, young believers, older mentors, even enemies?

GROUP WORSHIP (15-30 minutes)

The ultimate revelation of God's glory and the purest experience of worship will be at the consummation of history. That's when Jesus Christ will return and the heavenly Jerusalem will descend upon us.

22. Ask three volunteers to read the following selections from Revelation 21 aloud. The rest of the group should listen with eyes closed and imagine themselves in the picture. What would you see, smell, and feel as part of the scene? What does God's glory look like in its perfect state? After the reading is finished, take two minutes of silence to ponder it. Jot ideas below if that would be helpful.

☐ Revelation 21:1-4

☐ Revelation 21:10-11

☐ Revelation 21:22-27

23. Give everyone a chance to voice his or her responses to the period of silent meditation.

24. Worship in praise and in prayer as you perceive God in His glory. Bring music into your worship as appropriate and desired. Now would also be an appropriate time to do a responsive reading using one or more of the psalms that bid us to give God the glory due His name, such as Psalm 29, 57, 63, or 96.

4.
OUR RESPONSE TO GOD AND HIS GLORY

*To lift up the hands of prayer gives God glory, but a man
with a dungfork in his hand or a woman with a slop pail
gives Him glory, too. He is so great that all things give
Him glory if you mean they should.*
                    —*Gerard Manley Hopkins (1844-1889)*

OVERVIEW

God has taken the initiative to reveal Himself and His
glory to humans. We were created to reflect God's glory as if in a mirror,
but sin has clouded that mirror with smoke. God's redeeming grace,
which clears away that smoke and allows us to see God by faith, is but
the beginning or down payment of God's eternal glory. And God's eternal glory is the perfection of His grace available here and now.

In this session, we will look at several psalms and a passage from
Paul's letter to the Romans to see a variety of ways in which we can
respond to God's glory. These varied responses are called "worship."
Such worship entails all of life, not just our so-called prayer life. Your
goal will be to discern how God wants you to respond to His glory.

So what's the big deal?
Once we find out how God reveals His glory, and that He does so with
a loving, redemptive purpose in mind, we will want to respond appropriately. To respond less than adequately, in ways contrary to how God
designed us, does terrible damage both to individuals and to the soci-
ety in which we live.

The psalmists struggled to find words to express their devotion to God. Pay special attention to how their varied responses describe the interaction between God and His people.

1. List all the verbs in the following passages that express the human response to God's glory. (How many different ones can you find?) What do these expressions tell you about how the God-human relationship is supposed to work?

   ☐ Psalm 5:3

   ☐ Psalm 34:1-3

   ☐ Psalm 37:3-7

   ☐ Psalm 46:10

   ☐ Psalm 55:16-17

2. Project yourself into the various situations of the psalmists. What do you imagine prompted the particular responses to God's glory that you see in each case?

☐ The situation in Psalm 5:3:

☐ The situation in Psalm 34:1-3:

☐ The situation in Psalm 37:3-7:

☐ The situation in Psalm 46:10:

☐ The situation in Psalm 55:16-17:

☐ The situation in Psalm 69:30:

3. Which of the following are most typical of you?
   ☐ The habit of bringing your requests to God each morning.
   ☐ The faith to wait patiently on and expect great things from God.
   ☐ The offer of worship and exaltation in response to who God is.
   ☐ Thanking God in response to what He has done for us.
   ☐ Trusting God to make things right in the face of injustice.
   ☐ Submitting your desires to God, that He might fulfill them.
   ☐ Praying instead of worrying when adversity confronts you.
   ☐ Being still and not taking the initiative away from God.
   ☐ The no-holds-barred 911 call to God's helpline.

4. In which of these responses would you most like to grow?

5. Why do you suppose that response is hard for you?

6. We often think of worship as an activity confined to a few hours a week. But the apostle Paul makes it clear that worship is a whole life experience.

> Therefore, I urge you, brothers, in view of God's mercy, to offer your bodies as living sacrifices, holy and pleasing to God—this is your spiritual act of worship. (Romans 12:1)

What do you think Paul means when he says, "offer your bodies as living sacrifices"?

 GROUP DISCOVERY (50-90 minutes)

Let's Warm Up (10 minutes)

7. Recall your earliest memory of noticing or experiencing God's glory. What do you suppose God was trying to communicate to you at the time?

Let's Talk (30-50 minutes)

Paul began his letter to the Romans by describing the Roman Empire as he had observed it. Have someone in the group read Romans 1:18-25 aloud, while the rest listen for ways in which our modern world is similar.

8. What was wrong or inappropriate about the way the people were responding to God's glory (Romans 1:18-21)?

9. How did God judge them?
   - ☐ They reaped what they sowed.
   - ☐ God turned His back on them as they had done to Him.
   - ☐ God gave them what they wanted—in spades.
   - ☐ God let the law of natural consequences take over.
   - ☐ Other (please explain):

10. Why did God judge them as He did?

11. How have you observed people from your world responding to God's glory in ways as devastating as those described in Romans?

12. What do you think is our responsibility to others, both believers and non-believers, when we see them making the mistakes Paul describes?

☐ God is sovereign and we must leave all responsibility to Him.

☐ Since we are our brother's keeper, we may suffer the same fate if we fail to warn them.

☐ They're getting what they deserve and seemingly want, so why interfere?

☐ We should model the gospel, and if necessary use words, so that they will see our good works and give God the glory He deserves.

☐ Let the truth about God be known and combat all attempts to suppress it.

☐ Other (please explain):

13. What did you learn from the psalms you read about positive responses to God's glory?

Let's Act (15-30 minutes)

14. From your reading in Psalms and Romans, evaluate the ways you typically respond to God's glory in your heart, words, and deeds.

a. Describe a strength in your current response to God's glory. For example, *I'm quick to cry out to God when I'm in distress.*

b. What is one weakness in your response to God up to this point? For example, *I forget to express gratitude because I often focus on what's wrong with my life.*

15. As a result of your study so far, in what new ways will your group respond to God's revelation of His glory?

GROUP WORSHIP   (15-30 minutes)

16. Read through Psalm 23 aloud, one verse per person. After each verse is read, pause to identify or elaborate on the specific images David uses to describe his relationship with God. For example, someone might respond to the statement, "I shall not be in want [or lack]" (verse 1), by thanking God for having this month's house payment in hand. "The valley of the shadow of death" (verse 4) could remind someone of divorce, major illness, job termination, or some other traumatic loss. Thank God for His Shepherd-like provisions and protection of your sheep-like group.

17. Bring music into your worship. You could sing about Christ as our Shepherd.

18. Split the group into pairs for 10 minutes of prayer. Try to focus prayer primarily on requests to respond to God's glory more fully in whatever worship setting you find yourself in—at church, at home, at work, in the marketplace, throughout your daily life. Confess ways in which you have not been responding appropriately to God's glory. Also, pray for others you know who need to see and respond to God's glory.

Let's Listen to God (15 minutes)

Throughout this study guide the question, "What do you think the Holy Spirit is saying to your group about . . . ?" is raised. Perhaps it seems presumptuous to claim to know what the Spirit is saying. Perhaps you are confident that you know, or maybe you are willing to settle for what you think the Spirit *ought* to be saying to your group.

Listening to the Spirit's voice is a skill your group can develop over time. It requires discipline and the willingness to cultivate certain attitudes and take certain risks. As you begin your time of listening to God, read aloud the following commitments. These are not once-for-all-time commitments; each one will require a process of commitment and recommitment by each group member.

▶ We acknowledge our own agendas, plans, philosophies, ideas, and paradigms, and we determine not to let them interfere with our relationship with God or with each other. We may not get this right all the time, but will keep it in mind every week as we meet.

▶ We commit ourselves to being open, honest, vulnerable, available, and transparent. Of course, if we're going to do this for real, we will have to deal with the relationship tensions and conflicts that arise. The result will be the beginning of authentic relationships.

▶ We present ourselves to God in humility, poverty of spirit, brokenness, contrition, and submission. God says He is near to these kinds of persons (Isaiah 57:15, 66:2). The prophet Azariah told the king and people of Judah:

> "The LORD is with you when you are with him. If you seek him, he will be found by you, but if you forsake him, he will forsake you. For a long time Israel was without the true God. . . . But in their distress they turned to the LORD, the God of Israel, and sought him, and he was found by them." (2 Chronicles 15:1-4)

Your agenda for this time of listening to God is to try to hear what God is saying through each group member as you share your thoughts on the following questions. Your challenge is to listen to God while talking to each other. Take a moment for silent prayer, then spend about fifteen minutes on the following:

19. After reading aloud the preceding three commitments, discuss what you sense the Holy Spirit is communicating to your group about the following areas.

    ☐ Your worship and relationship with God

    ☐ Your relationships with each other

    ☐ Your relationships with those outside this group

Take a moment to close this conversation in prayer.

5.

BALANCING FREEDOM AND ORDER IN WORSHIP

Creation, which seems like pure freedom, involves limita-
tion. . . . Rebellion, which also seems like freedom,
involves limitation as well.

—Philip Yancey

OVERVIEW

The early Gentile church had no buildings, no denominations, no fixed organization, no New Testament, no vocabulary of its own, no dogmatic system, and no Sunday school. How did it then survive when it had none of the things that we now deem important?

Without traditions and established infrastructure, the earliest Christian communities were forced to depend upon the Holy Spirit for guidance in worship. As believers throughout the Roman Empire gathered in the name of Christ, many from pagan backgrounds, the apostle Paul instructed them in the basics of Christian worship.

One issue that arose was the balance of freedom and order. In his First Letter to the community at Corinth, Paul advocated forms of worship that maintained enough order to give the Spirit room to be fully active in the community's midst. This principle harmonized with what the Jewish church in Jerusalem had concluded several years earlier at a council described in the book of Acts.

In this session you will investigate how the church struggled to avoid shipwrecking either on suffocating controls or utter chaos. Your goal will be to find your own balance between Spirit-led freedom and Spirit-controlled order in worship.

So what's the big deal?

Most fellowships and worship traditions tend to lean too much toward freedom or too much toward control. If we fail to find the balance, we miss out on the depth of worship God wants for us.

ON YOUR OWN (30-60 minutes)

By the time of Jesus, centuries of worship had shaped Jewish practice. However, after the Resurrection and Pentecost, God's self-revelation in Jesus and the Holy Spirit shook the assumptions upon which Jewish customs were founded.

The Jewish Christians in and around Jerusalem transitioned gradually to distinctly Christ-centered worship. They maintained many aspects of temple and synagogue worship while reinterpreting its rituals and symbols according to their fulfillment in Christ. These believers instituted new practices such as the Lord's Supper that allowed them to focus their worship more fully on Christ. In addition, they supplemented the temple and synagogue worship with meetings in homes (Acts 5:42).

By contrast, Jewish Christians outside Palestine were less steeped in temple practices and more accustomed to Greek ways. Further, Gentile Christians had no interest at all in maintaining Jewish customs. They found Jewish dietary laws annoying, and they considered circumcision barbaric—bodily mutilation was unthinkable to the Greeks. Hence, they rejected many Jewish rituals and made a clear distinction between what was culturally Jewish and what was Christian. These distinctions caused conflict with the traditionalists.

Things came to head when some Jews from Palestine traveled to Paul's home base in Syrian Antioch to insist that the Gentile converts there conform to Jewish customs. Paul and Barnabas, leaders of the missionary efforts to the Gentiles, challenged that teaching. The two sides agreed to take the question to the leaders of the original community in Jerusalem.

1. In Acts 15:1-35, the physician Luke records a summary of what happened at that meeting in Jerusalem. What were the main issues that divided the two ethnic groups?

2. What did the leaders (Paul, Barnabas, James, Peter) see wrong with relying on the centuries-old tradition of circumcision?

3. Peter referred to this divide as "putting on the necks of the disciples a yoke that neither we nor our fathers have been able to bear" (Acts 15:10). James concluded, "We should not make it difficult for the Gentiles who are turning to God" (15:19). To what do you think this "yoke" or "difficulty" refers?

Eating food previously offered in pagan rites, blood, and meat of strangled animals (which was not drained of blood) was so contrary to Jewish food laws that Jews simply could not bring themselves to eat these things. An analogy might be if a group of Euro-American believers requested that believers from another culture not serve cat meat at shared meals.

4. If there is total freedom in Christ, and if salvation is through grace alone by faith alone, then why did the apostles and elders of the early church see the need to impose legal/moral requirements to order the worship life of the new converts (15:19-20,28-29)?

5. The Jerusalem Council of A.D. 49 considered the "burden" or "yoke" of circumcision to be a hindrance to the gospel, and thus dropped it as a membership requirement. A generation later, nobody worried about eating strangled chickens, and today Scottish Presbyterians eat blood sausage. So who's to say that some future General Assembly of believers will not find that the remaining religious traditions are passé? That is, if everything is by grace, then why does the church need any requirements?

6. What role did the Holy Spirit play in the decision-making process in Jerusalem?

7. What implications do you think this first council had for handling tradition among the followers of Jesus back then?

8. What implications do you think it has for us today?

 GROUP DISCOVERY   **(50-90 minutes)**

Let's Warm Up (10 minutes)

9. When have you attended a gathering where the worship style was considerably different from what you are used to? How did you feel at the time?

Let's Talk (30-50 minutes)

In Acts 15 you investigated a watershed agreement between two factions of the early church, each with drastically different views on tradition. The churches Paul founded in the Greek city of Corinth continued to struggle with how to organize Spirit-led worship. First Corinthians 14:26-40 comes at the end of Paul's long teaching on Spirit-led freedom and Spirit-controlled order in gatherings of believers. Have someone in the group read this passage aloud. Think about how your experience of worship is like, and unlike, what was apparently going on in Corinth.

10. Describe the scene in Corinthian worship services that you think Paul was reacting against.

11. What did Paul tell the Corinthians to do about ordering the following elements of worship?

☐ hymns, instruction, and revelation

☐ tongues and interpretation of tongues

☐ prophecy

☐ women asking questions during the meeting

12. What questions do Paul's instructions raise in your mind for how your group should operate when you gather together?

It would be easy to digress into discussing the role of prophets today, or debating how to reconcile Paul's instruction for women to be silent (14:34) with his statement a few chapters earlier that during the meeting women should cover their heads when they pray or prophesy (11:5). Without going into those important questions, focus instead on Paul's overarching principles regarding Spirit-led freedom and Spirit-controlled order.

13. How does the "Lord's command" (14:37) bring order and peace to worship without squashing the freedom to speak and prophesy?

14. What did you learn from Acts 15 about Spirit-led freedom and Spirit-controlled order?

15. How do your insights from 1 Corinthians 14 build upon what you learned in Acts?

Let's Act (15-30 minutes)

16. Strip away the social, economic, ethnic, cultural, denominational, historic, and traditional aspects of what you do when you gather together for worship. Imagine you are left with just the bare essentials for effective worship. What would that pure essence of worship look like? Sound Like? Feel like?

17. Examine your own small group in light of the biblical objective to balance Spirit-led freedom and order in worship. Which does your group tend to focus more on—freedom or order?

18. Based on what you have learned so far in this study, as well as from your experience and the resources in your group, design and use your own worship material for this session.

Let's Listen to God (15 Minutes)
As you begin your time of listening, read aloud again the commitments on page 50.

19. What is the Holy Spirit communicating to your group about the way it worships? For example, how can you improve your balance between freedom and order?

20. What is the Spirit saying to you about your relationships as a community? For example, the early believers experienced significant social, economic, ethnic, and cultural barriers that distracted and disrupted their worship life together. Are there any such barriers that interfere with people's freedom to worship God in your group?

21. What is the Spirit saying about your relationships with others outside your group?

22. Pray for the wisdom to balance freedom and order in the way you worship as a gathered group, and in the ways you respond to God's glory in the world.

6.

IDOLS OF THE HEART

The essence of idolatry is the entertainment of thoughts about God that are not worthy of Him.

—A. W. Tozer

OVERVIEW

God designed humans to worship Him in complete trust and serve Him by exercising dominion over His creation. When Adam and Eve sinned, they ruptured the harmony of this dynamic by displacing God from His rightful place in the innermost being of humankind. The race then began a search to fill the void left by God.

We have turned instead to false images, idols of our own making. The Bible describes man-made images as:

- ▶ detestable, abominable, shameful, and vile
- ▶ worthless and useless
- ▶ lifeless and mute
- ▶ manmade—cast, molded, or carved
- ▶ made of wood, stone, metal, gold, or silver

These qualities are so far removed from how the one living and true God is described that it is a wonder God's people ever fell for idols. But many people find manmade idols more convenient and controllable than God.

God's covenant prohibited all forms of idolatry (Exodus 20:3-5). Not only that, God's covenant with Israel warned about what would happen if Israel turned its heart away from God and toward idols

(Deuteronomy 30:17). Centuries later, after the Israelite kingdom divided in 922 B.C., all the kings of the north wandered into idolatry in one form or another, as did half the kings of the south.

You might conclude that idol worship was something primitive tribes did long ago in remote places. Not so. Idol worship takes on many modern, urban, and universal qualities. Not only houses, land, hobbies, and cars, but also folk heroes, loved ones, and prestigious networks can be idols. Even deeds done in the name of the Lord can become objects of our worship, and thus idols that displace God from the throne of our hearts.

Your goals in this session will be to explore why idolatry is so appealing, what consequences idolatry brings, and how your group can help you turn from idolatry.

So what's the big deal?
Most of us work hard to ignore and deny the idols we worship. But they are the chief obstacles keeping us from loving God well.

ON YOUR OWN (30-60 minutes)

Ezekiel spoke prophetically to God's people, predicting their destruction and exile if they continued in idolatry, then calling the exiles to repent by turning from idols to the living God.

1. Read Ezekiel 14:1-11. What does it mean to "set up idols in [one's] heart" (14:3,4,7)?

   ☐ We substitute dependence on God with dependence on people, possessions, and positions.

   ☐ Instead of exercising God's command to govern the created world, mankind cruelly dominates it.

   ☐ Our idols may not be carved, but are certainly craved—hobby horses, pet interests, sexual fantasies, addictions, or objects of fixation.

   ☐ If God is not at the center of our love life, then something or someone else is—and that is an idol.

   ☐ Other (please explain):

2. What did God promise to do to people who worshiped idols?

3. Why do you think God hates idolatry so much?

4. Idolatry has such a strong grip on the human heart that it demands drastic measures. What solution does God set forth in Ezekiel 11:17-21?

5. In Ezekiel 16, God compares Israel's worship of idols to an adulterous wife's prostitution of herself. Read Ezekiel 16:15-19. In what ways is idolatry like adultery and prostitution?

6. To which of the following modern-day idols are you most susceptible?
   - ☐ Ambition (I have an inordinate attachment to money, power, control, success, achievement, esteem, or self-sufficiency.)
   - ☐ Work (I tend toward workaholism, as I am strongly motivated by accomplishment, recognition, or promotion.)
   - ☐ Relationships (I have an inordinate attachment to my spouse, children, or another individual or group.)
   - ☐ Appetites (I have some appetites of the flesh I do not want to give up, such as food, sex, addictive behavior, power, or control.)
   - ☐ Material possessions (There are possessions I just can't do without, perhaps even an obsession with money or the lack of it.)
   - ☐ Ideas (Some ideas—political, religious or whatever—dominate my thought life, leaving little room for God.)
   - ☐ Activities (There are some things I do—exercise, movies, videos, music, recreation, sports—without which my life ceases to have meaning.)
   - ☐ Other idols:

7. Why are these things so appealing to you? What do they offer?

8. On the other hand, why is it so hard for you to view your habits as "adultery," "prostitution," "idolatry"—all such drastic forms of betrayal?

9. Is there anything you would like to say to God about these issues?

10. The biblical response to idolatry requires repentance and elimination of the prohibited idolatry. This may require a thorough and honest moral inventory of your heart. A trusted friend can support you in the process, pray with you for God's best, and remind you of your commitments. Whom in your group can you trust to tell about your struggle with idolatry? Write that person's name here.

 GROUP DISCOVERY (50-90 minutes)

Let's Warm Up (10 minutes)

Gordon Dahl, a Lutheran pastor, says modern Christians tend to "worship their work, work at their play, and play at their worship."

11. Recall the definitions of worship from session 2, page 26. In the family you grew up in, where did you experience the most worship, either God-centered or idolatrous?
    ☐ at work
    ☐ doing sports/leisure
    ☐ around the family altar
    ☐ at church
    ☐ on spiritual retreats
    ☐ other (please explain):

12. Currently, do you worship more in the context of work, sports and leisure, or a gathering of God's people?

The following text expands and applies the theme of idolatry without mentioning the word idol or idolatry.

> As they were walking along the road, a man said to him, "I will follow you wherever you go."
>
> Jesus replied, "Foxes have holes and birds of the air have nests, but the Son of Man has no place to lay his head."
>
> He said to another man, "Follow me."
>
> But the man replied, "Lord, first let me go and bury my father."
>
> Jesus said to him, "Let the dead bury their own dead, but you go and proclaim the kingdom of God."
>
> Still another said, "I will follow you, Lord; but first let me go back and say good-by to my family."
>
> Jesus replied, "No one who puts his hand to the plow and looks back is fit for service in the kingdom of God." (Luke 9:57-62)

13. An idol is something, someone, or some idea that defines self-identity, controls our life, and is the last thing we let go of. By this definition, what "idols" were these people who encountered Jesus in Luke 9 holding onto?

14. What idol does Jesus address in Luke 12?

> "Do not be afraid, little flock, for your Father has been pleased to give you the kingdom. Sell your possessions and give to the poor. Provide purses for yourselves that will not wear out, a treasure in heaven that will not be exhausted, where no thief comes near and no moth destroys. For where your treasure is, there your heart will be also." (Luke 12:32-34)

15. Why would Jesus say something as drastic as "sell your possessions"?

16. What feelings do Jesus' strong statements about family, home, and money stir up in you?

17. Why do you suppose these people were holding onto their idols, when the alternative that Jesus offered was such "good news"?

18. Imagine yourself in one of these situations in Luke 9 and 12, where Jesus challenges an "idol of the heart." Which one of these hits closest to home for you?

Let's Act (15-30 minutes)

19. How can a group like yours band together to combat idols in your hearts?

20. What risks are involved in seeking the help of others to combat your own idols?

21. Based on what you have learned about idolatry, as well as your experience and the resources in your group, design and use your own worship material for this session. You may want to incorporate elements of confession, private and public.

Let's Listen To God (15 Minutes)

As you begin your time of listening, read aloud again the commitments on page 50. Take adequate time for each member to share as much as he or she is able. You may want to plan an overtime session. You can encourage one another by sensitive questioning and by modeling appropriate levels of vulnerability and trust in your own sharing. Be sure to close in a round of prayer for each other, so that your sharing of concerns and your forsaking of idols is an act of obedience and worship before God.

22. What is the Holy Spirit saying to your group about worship through this session?

23. What is the Holy Spirit saying about your relationships with each other?

24. What is the Holy Spirit saying about your relationships outside the group?

25. Spend some time in prayer that God will replace your forsaken idols.

7.

FALSE WORSHIP
IN THE COMMUNITY

Man is a religious being; the heart instinctively seeks for a
God. Whether he worships on the banks of the Ganges,
prays with his face upturned to the sun, kneels toward
Mecca or, regarding all space as a temple, communes
with the heavenly Father according to the Christian creed,
man is essentially devout.

—William Jennings Bryan

OVERVIEW

The Old Testament tells story after story of people who
went astray from the one true God and began to pursue false gods. First
God entered into a covenant with His chosen people. This covenant was
like a marriage covenant in that it required His people to be faithful to
Him just as He had promised to be faithful to them. When God's people
wandered from Him to serve other gods, God called that adultery.

The nation of Israel was judged more harshly than its neighbors for
pursuing false religion because God's covenant people should have
known better, and they had ample opportunity to repent.

Likewise today, God's chosen people are prone to the subtle infil-
tration of false worship into our fellowships, and we are liable for the
consequences. Unless we are aware of what false worship looks like,
and how it appeals to so many, we too may succumb to its seduction,
not only individually (with "idols in our hearts") but corporately (with
false worship in the community).

Religious activity does not eliminate the danger of turning to idols. "Even while these people were worshiping the LORD, they were serving their idols" (2 Kings 17:41). We would be wise to engage in a little self-examination in light of Israel's history and propensity toward idolatry.

In this session you'll look at how idolatry, hypocrisy, apostasy, and human tradition can lead to false worship in the community. Your goal will be to assess what this means for your group.

So what's the big deal?

Just as the personal sin of idolatry calls for individual repentance, so the corporate sin of false worship calls for community-wide repentance.

ON YOUR OWN   (30-60 minutes)

People drift from true worship to false worship in various ways—through idolatry, hypocrisy, apostasy, and man-centered tradition. In Jeremiah 2:4-13, the prophet addresses idolatry.

Hear the word of the LORD, O house of Jacob,
    all you clans of the house of Israel.

This is what the LORD says:

"What fault did your fathers find in me,
    that they strayed so far from me?
They followed worthless idols and became worthless themselves.
They did not ask, 'Where is the LORD,
    who brought us up out of Egypt
and led us through the barren wilderness,
    through a land of deserts and rifts,
a land of drought and darkness,
    a land where no one travels and no one lives?'
I brought you into a fertile land
    to eat its fruit and rich produce.
But you came and defiled my land
    and made my inheritance detestable.
The priests did not ask, 'Where is the LORD?'

Those who deal with the law did not know me;
   the leaders rebelled against me.
The prophets prophesied by Baal,
   following worthless idols.
"Therefore I bring charges against you again," declares the LORD.
   "And I will bring charges against your children's children.
Cross over to the coasts of Kittim and look,
   send to Kedar and observe closely;
   see if there has ever been anything like this:
Has a nation ever changed its gods?
   (Yet they are not gods at all.)
But my people have exchanged their Glory
   for worthless idols.
Be appalled at this, O heavens, and shudder with great horror,"
   declares the LORD.
"My people have committed two sins:
They have forsaken me,
   the spring of living water,
and have dug their own cisterns,
   broken cisterns that cannot hold water." (Jeremiah 2:4-13)

1. How does Jeremiah describe idolatry in 2:11,13?

2. God had a wonderful plan for the Israelites, but they turned their backs on it. What was that plan?

3. Why did they find "worthless idols" and false gods so appealing?

4. What were the results of worshiping false gods?

Read Matthew 23:1-32 from whichever Bible version you prefer. In this passage, Jesus details the Pharisees' hypocrisy, or pretending to be one person on the outside when one is really someone else inside.

5. How does Jesus define or describe hypocrisy in the seven woes in Matthew 23? Pick one of the woes and explain how it shows hypocrisy.

6. How does hypocrisy undermine true corporate worship and lead to false worship?

In Matthew 24:10-13, Jesus speaks of apostasy, or turning away from one's faith in God.

"At that time many will turn away from the faith and will betray and hate each other, and many false prophets will appear and deceive many people. Because of the increase of wickedness, the love of most will grow cold, but he who stands firm to the end will be saved." (Matthew 24:10-13)

7. What results of turning away from faith does Jesus name in Matthew 24:10-13?

8. Why do people turn away from God?

9. What are the results of apostasy (individual and corporate, temporal and eternal)?

Read Mark 7:1-13. In this passage, Jesus critiques human tradition. When the Jews returned from exile in Babylon, the rabbis began to add traditional interpretations to the basic laws stated in the Torah (Genesis through Deuteronomy, the books of Moses). They collected the laws and traditions into 613 precepts. Considered part of the Torah, these precepts came to be as binding (in the minds of Jews) as the law of God itself. This collection of precepts is what Jesus referred to as "the traditions of the elders" or "the traditions of men" (Mark 7:2,8).

10. According to Jesus in Mark 7:1-13, what was wrong with this kind of tradition?

11. When people rely on their religious traditions to escape the clear implications of God's Word, what is Jesus' response?

12. What are some good aspects of religious tradition?

13. How can something essentially good be misused to promote false religion in the community, even today?

 GROUP DISCOVERY (50-90 minutes)

Let's Warm Up (10 minutes)

14. Choose one of the following questions to answer:

  a. What's something you've made with your own hands that you're really proud of?

  b. Who was your first "sweetheart?" Whatever happened to him or her? Is it possible or advisable to maintain friendship with former romantic interests?

Let's Talk (30-50 minutes)

15. What would be one biblical and one contemporary example of each?

  ☐ Idolatry

☐ Hypocrisy

☐ Apostasy

☐ Destructive Tradition

16. What would each of these kinds of false worship look like in a gathering of believers such as ours?

☐ Idolatry

☐ Hypocrisy

☐ Apostasy

☐ Traditions supplanting God's Word

One of the greatest tests of a community is its ability to honestly face and deal with its own idolatry, hypocrisy, apostasy, and destructive traditions. These are almost invariably blind spots for most or all of the group; people just aren't aware that one of their traditions violates God's Word, or they fail to notice themselves saying something very spiritual but doing the opposite. Few of us enjoy having these matters pointed out to us; we often become defensive or even hostile. Questions 17 and 18 test your ability to be honest first with yourself in private, and then with the rest of your group. See how well you can listen first to God and then to each other without defending yourselves against truth.

Let's Act (15-30 minutes)

17. Take five to ten minutes on your own to assess your group according to these four standards.

☐ I see no evidence of idolatry.
☐ Our group is idolatrous in these ways:

☐ I see no evidence of hypocrisy.
☐ We are hypocritical in these ways:

☐ I see no evidence of apostasy.
☐ Our group has fallen from the true faith in these ways:

☐ I see no evidence of traditions supplanting God's Word.
☐ We have the following traditions that contradict God's Word:

18. Compare your answers with those of others in the group. Discuss any differences. Try to listen carefully to one another.

19. Based on what you have learned about God being a jealous God—as well as your experience with idolatry, hypocrisy, apostasy, or tradition—design and use your own brief worship service for this session.

Let's Listen To God (15 Minutes)

As with the last session, take enough time for each member to share as much as he or she is able. Encourage one another by sensitive questioning and by modeling appropriate levels of vulnerability in your own sharing. Be sure to close in a round of prayer for each other, so that your sharing of concerns and your forsaking of idols is an act of obedience and worship before God.

20. Sometimes a whole city repents of sin, as did ancient Nineveh in response to Jonah's preaching. At other times a representative leader, such as the king of Israel, repents on behalf of the entire nation. Spend time in prayer to understand what God might want to reveal to you as a group. Psalm 139:23-24 may help you get started. Write down what comes to mind.

21. As a result of your discussion in this session, what do you feel the Holy Spirit is communicating to your group in these areas?

☐ Your worship and obedience to God

☐ Your need to repent of any false worship you've identified

8.

LET'S PERSONALIZE WORSHIP

In this session and the next, you will review and apply the lessons you have learned in sessions 2–7. In this session you will focus on personal lessons and applications, while session 9 will focus on group applications. As you prepare for your group meeting, remember to pray frequently. Some inventory work will help you select the one key truth from sessions 2–7 that is most urgent for you personally. Then your group will help you think through appropriate action steps and life changes you can pursue. Your goal will be to settle on one key truth and the action you can take to build it into your life.

So what's the big deal?

It's better to be obedient in just one area about which God is convicting you than to fill up a workbook full of good intentions about several truths, none of which you obey or profit from.

ON YOUR OWN   **(30-60 minutes)**

1. What changes are you beginning to see in your relationship with God as a result of this study?

☐ Any mistakes you are avoiding?

83

☐ Any attitudes you are changing?

☐ Any areas of new freedom in Christ?

☐ Any changes in the way you view God?

☐ Any new ways you feel or things you do when you spend time with God?

2. Review what you have studied and discussed in sessions 2 through 7. Try to state one or two truths that stand out to you as most important in each session. For example, for session 7 you might write, "It's better to be honest about our idols than hypocritical about them, pretending to worship God in public, while worshiping idols in private."

☐ Session 2

☐ Session 3

☐ Session 4

☐ Session 5

☐ Session 6

☐ Session 7

3. You may have repeated yourself in question 2, circling around the same one or two truths that jump out at you from every session. If so, it may be that the Holy Spirit has put His finger on an area of focus. Take a moment to pray about your list of truths. Put a star beside the one that you think is most important for you to address in the near future. Or, combine several of the truths into one, and state it below. (Don't get sidetracked trying to summarize all of your truths into one overarching thesis. The point is to pick one limited idea that you can reasonably grasp and focus on.)

4. How has this truth affected your thinking and behavior so far?

5. How do you think the Holy Spirit would like this truth to affect your life—your thoughts, feelings, and actions?

Be prepared to share your key truth and its effects with your group. They will help you formulate a plan for integrating that truth into your life and acting on it. They will also help keep you accountable to the degree that you allow them to do so. You're not in this alone!

 GROUP DISCOVERY (50-90 minutes)

Let's Warm Up (10 minutes)

6. What is one thing you have gained from this group during the past seven sessions? What is one thing for which you are grateful?

Let's Talk (45-80 minutes)

Plan your time so that you have at least five minutes for each person to share his or her truth and receive help in formulating a plan of action. Ten minutes each would be even better, but that might require going overtime. Be sure that no one is shortchanged of this opportunity for help.

7. Read to your group your key truth, how it has affected you so far, and how you think the Spirit would like it to affect you. Then, with help from the group, come up with a plan for integrating your key truth into your life. Ask yourselves the following questions as you help each other plan your strategies:

☐ Is the key truth clear?
☐ What results or outcomes would you like to see from this plan of action?
☐ Are the action steps specific and realistic?
☐ Not all action steps in the spiritual realm are quantifiable. For example, praying for thirty minutes a day is quantifiable, but genuinely opening your heart to God in prayer is not. How will you know if the changes you are pursuing are really happening?

Here is an example of a plan that is practical, specific, measurable, and clear:

I realize that I am letting work consume my life. Even when I try to become still before God, I find my thoughts straying to work. I don't make time for stillness very often either. So every day for the next month, I am going to take fifteen minutes at the end of my work day to sit in my car, read Revelation 4–5, and contemplate on what has been happening in heaven while I've been working. I'm going to tell God exactly what I'm feeling about my work at that moment, and I'm going to ask one question: "God, why do I let work consume my life?" When I get home, I'm going to call a friend from this group and leave a message on his answering machine about what came to me during that fifteen minutes. If I want to talk with him about it, I'll ask him to call me. My friend will remember to pray for me every day when he gets this message.

Write your plan here, continuing on the top of the next page:

8. List anything you have committed to do for someone else in your group:

9. Use this space to list the other group members' key truths (you will need these to do your personal preparation for session 9):

10. Design and implement your own time of worship. Be sure to include prayer about your key truth and your plans for applying it.

9.

LET'S GROW TOGETHER THROUGH WORSHIP

The work you do this session will be similar to session 8 in that you will review and apply the lessons you have learned in sessions 2–7. In this session your goal is to come up with an application for your whole group, whereas last time the focus was on personal application.

Planning group applications requires hard work. You will be thinking in areas that may be different from anything you have tried before. Six areas have been selected to help you evaluate your group's progress.

So what's the big deal?
If you persevere, you will achieve powerful results. You will be growing not just as individuals but also as a community of believers.

ON YOUR OWN   **(30-60 minutes)**

Throughout the course of these studies, you have had experiences that contributed to your sense of community. Take a few minutes to assess the progress and contributions your group has made in spiritual sensitivity, worship dynamics, relational intimacy, functional interdependence, mission focus, and sphere of influence. This assessment procedure will help you evaluate your group's progress and help you plan for your future relationships.

1. **Ability to listen to the Holy Spirit.** In a group with high sensitivity to the Spirit, you will observe unity and peace created by the Spirit, or you will observe people allowing the Spirit to disrupt their complacency and challenge their assumptions. On a scale of 1 (low) to 5 (high), how would you rate your group's sensitivity, receptivity, and responsiveness to the Holy Spirit's leadership?

1	2	3	4	5
low				high

2. **Worship dynamics.** God is the central focus in worship. Recall your worship times in the preceding sessions. In a group with "rich" worship dynamics you can expect to find a sense of God's majestic presence with you, variety, and everyone participating and contributing. On a scale of 1 (poor) to 5 (rich), how would you assess the overall quality of your group's worship experience?

1	2	3	4	5
poor				rich

3. **Relational intimacy.** The Bible is full of relational terms such as love, forgiveness, acceptance, reconciliation, and bearing one another's burdens. As you experience these conditions, your group will grow in relational intimacy. Evidences of "deep" intimacy are high levels of trust, vulnerability, transparency, honesty, and mutual commitment. On a scale of 1 (shallow) to 5 (deep), how would you assess your group's level of intimacy?

1	2	3	4	5
shallow				deep

4. **Functional interdependence.** The church is the body of Christ, a living organism with many members. Your small group functions like a system in that body, working interdependently with other systems and their members. Not only that, each member of your group is gifted to perform specific tasks that contribute to the overall internal functions of your group. On a scale of 1 (harsh, grating) to 5 (sweet, synchronized), how well are the members of

your community working together toward a common task, and how harmoniously is your community working alongside others?

1	2	3	4	5
harsh, grating				sweet, synchronized

5. **Mission focus.** Christian communities can easily become self-absorbed. This happens when they turn a deaf ear or a blind eye to what's on God's heart and, instead, focus their attention on themselves. The result is a diminished heart for the world that God loves and gave His Son to die for. God uses groups to reach into every nook and cranny of the world. On a scale of 1 (self-absorbed) to 5 (other-focused), how motivated is your group to looking beyond itself and fulfilling God's mission to reach the world?

1	2	3	4	5
self-absorbed				other-focused

6. **Sphere of influence.** God's mission is global in scope, including all kinds of people—rich and poor, men and women, young and old, Black, White, Hispanic, Asian, et cetera. Although we are to be open to new ministry opportunities, God often calls a community to minister within its specific sphere of influence. This sphere sets limits that sharpen your focus. On a scale of 1 (confused, non-existent) to 5 (sharply focused), how clear is it to your community who God has called you to minister to?

1	2	3	4	5
confused				focused

7. Review all the truths and life applications that you and your fellow group members identified last time. What is the one truth from these studies that you feel is most relevant for your whole group collectively? (This may be different from what is most significant to you personally.)

GROUP DISCOVERY (50-90 minutes)

Let's Warm Up (10 minutes)

8. What has been your most meaningful worship experience in this small group?

Let's Talk (30-45 minutes)

9. Share progress on personal applications from the last session. Are you helping each other follow through on your commitments? How so? Thank God for the progress He has already made among you.

10. Remember, community building is a process. Some members of your group may desire greater intimacy, and some may feel threatened by the intimacy already achieved. God is still at work in your group in the six areas you assessed on pages 90-91. He is molding you into a vehicle fit for Him to use however He wills. Review the six areas of assessment and compare answers as a group. Pay special attention to major differences in your evaluations. How do you account for these differences?

11. Discuss what each of you thinks is the one significant truth most relevant to your group (identified in question 7). Try to come to a group consensus of the one truth and its implications for your group. To reach that consensus, here are some helpful hints:
    - [ ] Begin with prayer, asking God to clarify your thinking.
    - [ ] List the truth from each individual on a chart or white board.
    - [ ] Look for duplications and related themes. Consolidate and combine where possible.

☐ Build consensus on one truth. Sometimes related thoughts can be combined to better reflect the overall truth but beware of stringing ideas together into a broad, complicated conglomeration.

☐ Don't worry about a perfect statement. Blend the ideas of each person in the group to arrive at the consensus position. (Designate someone in the group who has an aptitude with words to edit for clarity and length. Take the statement home to polish it up, if necessary.)

12. Write your group truth here.

13. Next you will plan how to integrate this truth into your group life, much as you did for each individual group member last time. Your first step will be prayer. Take five minutes to ask God to lead you in this process. You might ask, "Lord, how would you like our group to put this truth into practice?" or "God, what would you like our community to become?" Listen quietly. As you have thoughts or impressions, either make mental notes or jot them down.

14. Write three headings on newsprint or a white board: God, One Another, Others. Under the first heading, list ways in which this truth should affect your group's relationship with God. Under the second heading, list ways in which this truth should affect your relationships with each other, and so on.

God	One Another	Others

15. Now brainstorm a fourth list: things you can do to put this truth into practice in your group. Call out ideas without evaluating or criticizing any of them.

16. After five or ten minutes, stop and sort the ideas into short-range steps and long-range steps. Edit them so that each one is a realistic, doable action that lends itself to accountability. Who will do what, by when, where, and for/with whom? Weed out any impractical ideas. Try to come up with at least one short-range and one long-range step that meet these standards.
    - ☐ What is it?
    - ☐ Who will do what?
    - ☐ By when?
    - ☐ Where?
    - ☐ For/with whom?

    a. Short-range steps

    b. Long-range steps

Because learning to implement this truth as a community is so important, you should commit yourselves to take as many sessions as needed to work out your group application. Place a higher priority on implementing your plan rather than moving on to another study.

GROUP WORSHIP   (15-30 minutes)

17. Design and implement your own time of worship. Be sure to include prayer about your key truth and your plans for applying it. Also, thank God for what you have received from this study. Celebrate your time together, both your past and your future.

If you set out to identify the core elements of the Christian life, what would your list include?

After ten years of Bible study involving thousands of believers from countries all around the world, The Navigators' SCRIPTURAL ROOTS OF LIFE team saw a few basic themes emerge over and over again:

WORSHIP
Worship: Honoring God in All of Life
(ISBN: 1-57683-007-1; 9 sessions; 96 pages)

COMMUNITY
Relationships: Resolving Conflict and Building Community
(ISBN: 1-57683-023-3; 9 sessions; 96 pages)

INTIMACY WITH GOD
Intimacy: Pursuing Intimacy with God
(ISBN: 1-57683-010-1; 9 sessions; 96 pages)

BECOMING LIKE CHRIST
Christlikeness: Committing Ourselves to be Changed by God
(ISBN: 1-57683-006-3; 9 sessions; 96 pages)

THE TRINITY
Restoration: Discovering How God Meets Our Deepest Needs
(ISBN: 1-57683-009-8; 9 sessions; 96 pages)

THE UNSEEN WORLD
Warfare: Discovering the Reality of the Unseen World
(ISBN: 1-57683-026-8; 9 sessions; 96 pages)

SHARING THE FAITH
Outreach: Sharing the Real Gospel with the World
(ISBN: 1-57683-012-8; 9 sessions; 96 pages)

WORK
Work: Serving God on the Job
(ISBN: 1-57683-024-1; 9 sessions; 96 pages)

Designed to foster close-knit community within your group, the FOUNDATIONS FOR CHRISTIAN LIVING series is a great way to grow strong in faith, life, and love for God. Available at your local Christian bookstore. Or call 1-800-366-7788 to order.

NAVPRESS
BRINGING TRUTH TO LIFE